The Kindly Interrogator

Alireza Abiz

THE KINDLY
INTERROGATOR

translated from Persian by
W.N. Herbert & Alireza Abiz

Shearsman Books

First published in the United Kingdom in 2021 by
Shearsman Books Ltd
PO Box 4239
Swindon
SN3 9FN

Shearsman Books Ltd Registered Office
30–31 St. James Place, Mangotsfield, Bristol BS16 9JB
(this address not for correspondence)

www.shearsman.com

ISBN 978-1-84861-770-4

Contents

Introduction

Alireza Abiz belongs to the '90s generation of Iranian writers, who pioneered a literary revival in the wake of the Islamic Revolution and the eight years war with Iraq. The poetry of this generation is informed by postmodern literary theory and is marked by new experiments with both language and form.

The origins of modern Persian poetry are found in the constitutional revolution of 1906 and the intellectual movements before and after that historical landmark, which brought Persian poetry into the forefront of social struggle. Poets used poetry as a vehicle of protest and enlightenment, deploying elements of everyday language in an effort to make poetry more accessible to the masses. Cultural interactions with the West and translations of Western literature started to influence Persian poetry. Modern concepts entered classical forms, and gradually the forms themselves changed to accommodate modern approaches.

Nima Yushij, called the father of *She'r Noe* (New or Modern Poetry), is considered the first significant poet who advocated a form similar to blank verse at the turn of the twentieth century. He believed that Persian classical poetry had been too abstract, subjective, and metaphysical, and advocated a more objective approach and natural diction. His followers developed his ideas and introduced free verse and prose poetry.

In the 1960s the movement that Nima started reached its pinnacle, and some of the best known modern poets, including Forugh Farrokhzad, Mehdi Akhavan Saleth, Ahmad Shamlou and Sohrab Sepehri, published their works. Different movements followed and free verse in diverse styles and schools became the mainstream form of poetry writing.

Modern Persian poetry was strongly involved with social and political issues, and advocated idealistic visions of freedom and equality. Many poets were involved in political struggles and were prosecuted for their writings both before and after the 1979 Revolution. After the revolution and due to the eight year war, publication of literature suffered, but in the 1990s, poetry experienced a new revival.

In today's Iran, various post-modern styles live side by side with centuries old classical poetry – which has itself diversified into numerous branches, such as post-modern *ghazal*, progressive *ghazal*, ritualistic poetry, and so on.

Abiz's generation experienced major social and political upheavals. As a child, he experienced the revolution which replaced a 2,500-year old monarchy system with the Islamic Republic, a then unique new form of government.

As a teenager, he was consumed with revolutionary and religious fervour and volunteered for the front line when he was 16. In the 1980s, Iran was an extremely gloomy place with huge pressure being placed on any political dissent. There were constant processions mourning victims of the war, and social freedoms were non-existent. The reforms of the 1990s offered a glimmer of hope for democracy and a lively intellectual atmosphere, but prosecution and censorship continued, leading to a new wave of migration, especially after the 2009 uprising. Many poets left Iran and chose a life in exile.

Although Abiz doesn't consider himself an exiled poet, he is nevertheless influenced by the group experience of exilic literature. His poetry touches on all his personal experiences of living, studying and working in these turbulent times and the major social upheavals in his home country.

His work has what feels to an English language reader like a unique but not entirely unfamiliar texture which you could classify as a dialled-down or even buttoned-up surrealism. Extraordinary, terrible things appear to be happening – his speakers move between life and death, and between victim and torturer or even murderer – but no-one, least of all the poet, seems to draw attention to the fact. The impact of his work depends on this extreme tension between the calm of its surface and the unfathomable uncertainty revealed to occupy its depths.

This is of course a response to living and writing under a repressive regime in which, as he has eloquently explored in his study, *Censorship of Literature in Post-Revolutionary Iran* (I.B.

Taurus / Bloomsbury, 2021), censorship and its consequences are so universal as to become deeply internalised, and where your censor might – almost – seem like your most insightful reader. This deeply unsafe space, where words or gestures can betray you with terrible consequences, and where almost no-one, not even yourself, can be entirely trusted, has had a radical effect on his poetry and the poetry of his generation.

'The book is illuminated by the, properly, tragic insight that, in a world constructed along lines of absolute right and wrong, while it can become tragically clear at any moment who is the perpetrator of oppression, the corrupting influence of dogmas is so insidious that no-one remains entirely innocent, or, if carried along by the paranoias of ideological purity, should be considered completely guilty. It is an insight of immediate relevance to the polarising factions of liberal democracy, which presume themselves capable of right and even righteous thinking, but who are therefore lulled by the seemingly permanence of their governing structures into imagining themselves immune from precisely this temptation toward unequivocality. Our humanity, it implies, lies in our doubt, and, most especially, in our self-doubt.'

There are parallels here with the Chinese poets of the Menglong or 'Misty' generation, where, during the 1980s, there was recourse to imagery and literary techniques which the censors would find obscure (or doubtful), but which their readers gave themselves permission to puzzle over and identify with. Then, post-Tiananman, there was a second phase in which these techniques were reapplied in various conditions of actual or internalised exile, where the audience more obviously included the rest of the world. So Abiz combines in this volume poems written from both inside and outside Iran. Like the work of those poets, and of other writers who have had to keep themselves at least one step smarter than their persecutors, layers of coded allusion both to an ominous present and a rich literary heritage acquire a type of allegorical significance in which symbols of freedom or oppression – doves, rabbits, ghouls, lemons, feasting, wine – acquire disquieting lives of their own.

Similarly, ordinary addresses accrue sinister import through repetition, and are discovered to be sites of torture and interrogation. The precise cut of a beard reveals the oxymoronic 'kindly interrogator' of the title poem, and, throughout the poems written in exile, there is a sense that Iran both as malign regime and as nostalgic homeland can never be truly left. The dichotomy between these aspects, it seems, remains unresolved, and must be carried with the poet, haunting everything he sees, hears, and writes.

The final sensation, paradoxically, is one of liberation through insight: the poems obsessively revisit traumatic scenes, but come to control their perspective. They find unexpected insight into the torments of the tormentors, subjecting them to imaginary reparations, and experience an all-encompassing compassion as well as discovering untouched moments of resistance and liberation: a soldier on the front line at dawn, the recollection of a verse by Eliot, the peace of a garden bench. It is a tribute to the intense, contained energies of Abiz's imagination that the reader too experiences both the strange complicities of living in oppression and the genuine redemption that this poetry strives for throughout.

The Kindly Interrogator

The Tired Soldier

From behind many hills
the wail of jackals wakens me
and the futile voices of the dawn.

Bugles cough like sick roosters
and the morning sun
bursts through the needles
of the garrison's pines.

The tired soldier
hangs his boots around his neck
and pisses in his helmet.

My ID Card

The agent asked me for an ID card
and none of my cards had a photo
so I had to talk to the woman passing outside in the street.
The woman fell down
and was transformed into a blade of grass.

Terrified, I returned.
The agent still had my card, photo-less, in his hand.
We went out into the street,
the woman was passing, her handbag over her shoulder.

I called out to her.
She turned and, in the form of a lifeless dove,
descended onto my ID card.

The Black Cat

For a long time now, this black cat
has been sitting outside on my veranda
with his eyes shining,
looking at me through the darkness.

It's been a long time since I was a sparrow,
since I was a dove,
even since I was a backyard hen.

But still this black cat
is sitting on the veranda outside my room
with his eyes shining,
looking at me through the darkness.

Detention

The heater was swallowing both our shivers
and the jug of gas oil,
and its smoke in the half-dark cellar
went up to help the spiders.

A middle-aged man was laughing joyously,
he had killed his neighbour.
An old man, fingers trembling,
put a cigarette between yellow teeth
while eyeing the teenage boy
who was singing in a sad voice.

A young man swept slowly
he had long fingers
and had been brought in drunk from the gutter.

I had only written on the wall
Safoora, my darling,
my red rose, I'd die for you.

The Café

We came out of the café at five
for a short walk in the street.
For a short walk in the street
we came out of the café at five.

A man kept shaking his head
in the butcher's on the right.
In the butcher's on the right
a man kept shaking his head.

When at five they beheaded us
we also shook our heads.
We also shook our heads
when at five they beheaded us.

The Ship

The ship stood by the shore
and the one-eyed captain went on deck.
A huge fire could be seen on the beach
and in the cathedral bells were tolling.

We thought the ship was burning
and threw ourselves into the water in terror.
The fire was still ablaze on the shore
and the natives were dancing around.

We were in the ship and the ship was in us.

Puberty in the Trenches

Fall in!
You stand in line in Palangân Mosque
your knapsack being filled
with tins of tuna and gifts of nuts.
Magazine pouches ornament your waist.
Fall in!
In a long queue you climb Mount Shâhoo
listening to the breeze through the grass
and the river flowing down in the valley.

Sit behind that boulder
and let the river below pass through the valley.
The men carry water in white containers.
Sit behind that boulder
and aim at the bull's-eye –
Fire!

Spring grass is being crushed underfoot.
It has covered the graves,
and the moustaches of Akbar Komoleh.
Forward!
Your boots are too big for your feet.
When you turn the first corner
you see Dervish Faaress
with his long carbine
rolling a cigarette.
You're scared –
grip your M-1 tightly

In your Israeli-made sleeping bag
you sleep comfortably with no report of guns.

In your wet dream
you've been left behind
by the company which has gone up to the front line.

In the tamarisk bushes
with a tin of hot water
I wash my body for the sake of Ghusl Janabat.
It's an obligation for me to purify, to get close to Allah!

'The Love Song of J. Alfred Prufrock'

'The Love Song of J. Alfred Prufrock'
comes to mind when I think of the hunchback who
under the mulberry in the alley by the mosque
would blow on his tea in the saucer
and take a fingertip of snuff from a little bottle,
facing the small bazaar where a girl in a white veil was passing.

Since Saturday evening he has squatted behind his door
like a dog curled up by the side of the road
who neither barks nor howls
Just gnaws at the core of your soul with his eyes.

'The Love Song of J. Alfred Prufrock'
when he goes down four steps
so as not to see his mother washing other people's clothes,
and goes up two other steps
to get back to checking on the neighbour's roof.

Azan is called,
in the small bazaar
women slowly come and go
talking of Michelangelo.

Private Library

The books feel at home in the private library,
they loll on the shelves
and gossip endlessly.
They mix in no order and without discipline,
when a new book arrives
they conspire to kick it out.

In that corner
The Collected Works of Marx
is staring open-mouthed and besotted
at *Madame Bovary*.

To Shâh Cherâgh Shrine, All My Lemons

Reassure me, reassure me, oh God!
Doesn't remembering You reassure all hearts?
I was picking lemons, picking lemons in the garden,
dropping them into my lap,
the hem of my dress in my teeth.
My navel was showing, oh God, my navel was showing,
and a little below, a little above.
A breeze was blowing on my newly-ripened body
up to my armpits.
I was picking lemons, dropping them into my lap.

The breeze was swirling about my body,
entering by my sleeves
leaving by my neckline.
I was picking lemons, dropping them into my lap.

The breeze was blowing up my legs
swirling about my thighs
chilling my young buttocks.
I was picking lemons, dropping them into my lap

I wanted the gardener to come
or the gardener's horse.
The watchman to come
or the watchman's dog.
Reassure me, reassure me, oh God!

The Leopard's Dream

I dream I've swallowed an oak tree
and its branches are spreading in my stomach.
Soon it will grow out of my skin.
A dove is building a nest on a bough
and a leopard is napping in the shadow of the tree.
In the leopard's dream
I am his mother and I'm suckling him.
I want to wake up, but
I'm afraid I may disturb the leopard's dream.

The Informer

I too was invited
to the ceremony for selecting the finest informer.

I wore my best shirt,
my shiny black shoes,
and my Italian suit.
I put on a tie and I used cologne.

Inside the hall, the presenter was on the podium.
All the candidates were left outside.
All the seats had already been taken
by the officers responsible for informing on the ceremony.

I Am That Fox

I am that fox
who stole between your vines
and devoured your grapes.

Take me to your cellar
and store me with your 7-year old vats.

Guardian of the Faith

I jumped out from behind the rock, barred his way and cried
Halt! Hands Up!
I searched his pockets, found nothing, shouted
Halt! Hands Up!
I took him in, laid him down, rolled him up, and stuck him to
       the wall
I searched his shoes and socks, found nothing, shouted
Halt! Hands Up!
I searched him from head to toenail, I searched the inside of
       his pants
the roof of his mouth, the corner of his eye, the hole of his arse.
I extracted blood from his veins, tissue from his muscles,
grey cells from his brain and neurons from his nerves.
I removed his balls and fried them in a pan.
I searched through his mind with a magnifying glass and found
       nothing.
That heretic had hidden his dirty thoughts somewhere else.
Somewhere a short distance above his head or about his body
in an aura that I could and could not see.
He glanced at me, grinned and was gone.
I was left standing there, like a guardian of the faith.

Love Letter from Sydney

The first epistle rises out of the broken parts of the ship
and from the tumult of the seabirds
in a turbulent night,
from among the bare bodies on cool sands,
Maroubra Beach, Malabar Beach, Bronte Beach,
and (does it taste French?) La Perouse,
who stands on the deck and shouts: *La Terre! La Terre!*
and another world is born.
And the first epistle takes form
from shingle and starfish
and the naked voice of waves at night,
and the wandering souls of sailors
which with each wave
are pounded on the shore and repelled.
And the black flags with broken skulls prowl the seas,
one-eyed thieves
hide the treasures of the world on unseen islands.
New islands take form,
lands are born
and like little warts
sit on the body of the ocean.

A weekly ticket
and a walk round the harbour
among the couples strolling from one café to another
for whom the pillars of bridges and the corners of walls
are poles and curtains
and the park grass
is a wedding bed
– with the permission of Captain Cook –
Amigo, amigo, amigo

And the wave of the crowd with the scent of Parisian perfume
and the sweat of women who have danced till dawn
– with the permission of Captain Cook –
and empty beer cans floating in the canals.

The first epistle comes to an end
and a taste remains in the mouth
from a good night's drinking
from an ongoing vertigo of voices and laughter.
Hurrah!

Stop! We have to get off.

The Anatomy Hall

There is a lamp on in the Anatomy Hall.

Standing on tiptoe I can see through the window.
The table in the middle and the quick movement of hands.
There is silence, the sound of my breath,
and the one bent over the table in the hall.

Standing there I can see him craning his neck.
Outside the window,
I see his fear, the sound of his breath,
and the flash of the knife in the dim light of the hall.

He bends over my head and smiles,
looking at me like a butcher looks at a carcass.

On the table in the middle of the hall,
relaxed, I sleep.

The Night Behaves Differently Toward Me

The night behaves differently toward me
since yesterday when I came to the world
as if I had never been here before.

Where did I come from yesterday to this world
that I should be treated differently?

Since yesterday
it takes me away, it brings me back,
it grips me, shakes me
and casts me off,
it spins me around
and drives me away.

It walks me down the hallway, on the cold carpet, on the cold brick.
It tears me apart, warp from weft,
ancestor from offspring.

I see a camel in the darkness,
her hump, her neck, her eyes.
The world is a dark corridor.

I wish I were a camel in this world,
I might have been treated differently.

My Pear Tree

My pear tree was stripped naked
in the wind and snow of November.
Rotting apples dropped in the yard.
A flock of birds crossed the sky.

In the desert, with wings wide open,
the birds glide smoothly.
The sky is clear blue, dotted with white clouds.

I want that desert and those birds
and to be seven years old
on the vast plain of Khorasan.

Another Chance

All winter I have thought of death.
All winter is too short to think about death.
My body is full of death,
death flows in my veins.
My blood, my lymph is composed of death,
death runs in me.
I see her in the movement of my muscles,
in the opening and closing of my eyelids,
in the shedding of my hair,
in the growth of my nails.

I lift a cup of tea to my lips,
in its pleasant warmth
is a secret delight.
A secret delight I have borrowed from death.
Beyond this winter
trees are drowned in blossom,
the spring breeze blows in my hair.
Death, with an affectionate smile on her lips,
gives me another chance.

The Young Rabbit

I left the house at night following a young rabbit.
She took me through the trees toward the sea.
A fierce wind blew and a sudden rain fell.
I stood on an esplanade and looked out at sea.
The rabbit was moving off on a shining board.
The sea was terrifying and I was shaking.
The rabbit was still moving away on the board.

I said nothing about my dream to you.
I said nothing about my dream to her.
I went back home from the sea, hopeless.
The rabbit was sleeping soundly in my bed.

The Writer's Study

The writer's study is dim in the light of dawn
– the curtains are closed –
he should have opened them – he hasn't.
If I were the writer
I would have thrown open the curtains
unlatched the window
invited the light into the room.

I am not the writer
only the scribbler of these lines.
Out of extreme idiocy
I have drawn the curtains
on this beautiful morning.
I am sitting in the kitchen
staring at a can of salt on the table.

'The whole of existence frightens me'
Kierkegaard

In the wind there was a strange desire,
a pulsing urge to blow.
It wanted to blast and to endure.
In me there is a similar desire,
a beating urge to survive
and stir up the sea,
and create tall unending waves,
and shatter ramshackle walls.

A high desire which helps me overcome
my fear of existence.

Pilgrims

Pilgrims pass along mountain roads,
through plantations and across pastures,
across the infertile deserts,
over the rivers and over the seas.
They pass through the forests and through the woods.

They pass by sleeping sailors.
They pass by tired harvesters.
They pass by dogs and they pass by sheep.

They are always on the road.
In every city they have a street in their name,
an inn, a monastery, a temple.
They are forever on the road
from one pilgrimage site to another
in a continuing bewilderment
which will not end until they themselves
become a new pilgrimage site.

Red and White Domes
(Paul Klee)

Red and white domes,
blue and turquoise domes,
mud-brick and clay domes.

These domes,
grown everywhere across the earth,
their beauty is so motherly,
their curve so feminine.
They haven't raped the sky,
they have crept into it slowly and softly.
They have slept like a dream on the bed of air.
When you look down from the sky,
the earth looks like a thousand-breasted cow
with domes of red and white, blue and turquoise, brick and clay.
Under the ceilings of these domes,
life flows like warm milk in the veins of time.

The Bridge

You will cross the bridge in vain.
Nothing is happening on the other side.
On the other side your brother is dead
and his men have fled to the forest.

The bridge ends when you cross the bridge.

The Shepherds' Song

I was speaking to the tree in the night
of the happy days which are endless.
The sun was shining on the flowers.

I went down the alley between the gardens.
A piercing pain enveloped me.

Blood was springing from my hands,
I was whistling a shepherds' song.

The child remained in the gardens.
I went out of the alley.
At home,
there was talk of the gardens and the alley.

I am on fire, my body is burning.
I leave my flesh, and creep into you.

A White Bird

I come home by myself.
My wife is not in – she's gone.
I take the water bottle out of the fridge – it's empty.
I put a glass under the tap,
black smoke emerges.
A ghoul takes shape.
It looks into my eyes
with two burning coals,
claps me on the shoulder saying:
My friend!
It hasn't rained here for ages.
Stay thirsty for today,
tomorrow will be cloudy.

I went out into the street after her.
Distraught, I went after her.
Ecstatic, she was fleeing on the back of a white bird.

The Kindly Interrogator

I have a kindly interrogator.
He's interested in philosophy and free verse.
He admires Churchill and drinks green tea.
He is delicate and bespectacled.
He is lightly-bearded and has a woman's voice.
He is polite and doesn't insult me.
He has never beaten me up.
He has never demanded false confessions.
He says: *only write the truth.*
I say: *on my life!*

Umbrella

I opened the door to her,
invited her in.
She closed her umbrella and entered.

She sat on a chair,
I brought tea.
We smoked,
talked about the weather and politics.

I led her to the bathroom,
sliced her into small pieces,
placed her in the freezer.

Her umbrella is hanging from the coat rail.

The Island

I wish there were a way to that island,
a wooden bridge to pass over these weeds
and between those white swans and ducks.
A bridge I could walk across,
and lean upon its rail
to look at my reflection in the water of the lake
in this hand-knitted hat
with this beautiful face
that I have brought from the Khorasan plains
to here.

Now That I Am Dead

Now that I am dead,
I am the same as that runner or this jumper,
as one who watched over his body for his whole life
or another who exercised three times a day.

Now that I am thrown here
onto this slab in the mortuary,
look at me.
I am the same as the corpse beside me.
Perhaps more gaunt,
eyes more sunken,
but if you look closely
we are the same
we are both dead.

In My Dream

In my dream I saw a meadow of violets.
In my dream I saw a white calf.
In my dream I saw a harvested field.

In my dream I saw a pregnant hen
In my dream I saw a blind child.
In my dream I saw a rifle regiment.

A harsh rain fell.
I was a half-eaten crust in a sparrow's mouth.

The Fly

I chased the fly out of the kitchen.
He will die tonight.
I opened the door onto the yard,
and, many times, I shooed him out with the yellow napkin,
and each time he came back in.
In a small saucepan on the stove,
I was cooking black-eyed beans.
The fly flew toward the pan,
drinking in the steam from the beans.
I swatted at him with the napkin,
careful not to hit him –
I don't want his blood on my hands.
He made a turn and hid under the table.
I could easily have grabbed him.
I was scared I would catch germs and kill the fly as well.
I don't want his death to be at my hand.

I chased him out with the yellow napkin
and quickly closed the door.
If I want to have a smoke in the yard
I must remember to shut the door after me.
If the fly were smart
he would go and sit on that vent – is it from the boiler?
There's always warm steam there.
I don't think he is that intelligent,
and I wouldn't know how to explain this to him.
And anyway, he's not going to last the winter is he?

My Daily Schedule

On the notice-board, there is a photo of a poet
who died when he was fifty,
and beside it, the poster for *The 400 Blows*,
which I saw at the cinema last Thursday.
To the right of this poster,
an invitation to a poetry reading in the botanic gardens.
Beneath it, the instructions for operating the Venetian blinds,
And, beside those, the recycling schedule.

In the centre is my daily schedule.
According to this, I am now asleep.
At 11:00 hours, I have breakfast.
At 13:00 hours, I translate.
At 15:00 hours, I am in the library.
At 19:00 hours, I do whatever I like.

For a few years now, I have resided at 19:00 hours.

'Worthy is the lamb who was slain'
(Revelations: 5,12)

The fog is coming toward me from the end of the alley,
from the corner where a gate stands half-open.
It engulfs the black Ford and the red Honda,
creeps on and slowly fills the alley.
It climbs the hedges and the walls,
swallows the houses opposite one by one
until only the chimneys are visible.
It stands in front of me like a wall,
curls around the tree facing my window.
I open the window.
The fog embraces me.
I close my eyes and with thousands of other ghosts
I am carried away.

The Little Window

I would like to live long enough
to go back one day to Mashhad,
to 13/1 Koohsangee Street.
To knock at the little window
for the green-hatted Sayyed to open the door.
To go in,
sit facing the wall in the room to the left.
See *This too shall pass* on the wall.
And, while filling in sheet after sheet,
for once to turn around and without permission
look into your eyes!

Plain of Paradise

I've been invited to a wedding party in Dasht-e-Behesht –
does this mean anything to you?
I've been invited to a wedding party in Hotel Evin –
does this mean anything?

When the waiters in frock coats and white gloves
place large dishes of lamb and pilau on the table,
when the battle of forks and plates breaks out
on the long table as the guests move round –

what is happening next door?
On the other side of this wall? Under these watchtowers?

Things

I have many things

glass	teapot	sugar bowl
table	chair	central heating
gas oven	dishwasher	fridge-freezer
socket	napkin	ashtray
dining room	sitting room	kitchen
staircase	bathroom	bedroom
sheet	pillowcase	blanket
toaster	coffee maker	ironing board

I don't have human rights,
freedom, a happy heart.

Full-Length Mirror

I would like to live long enough
to go back one day to Mashhad
to 13/1 Koohsangee Street.
To see you come out of the gate
in the same dark glasses.
To see the corner of your eye,
which looks as if it has been sutured.
To follow your car to your door,
see you put the key in the lock
and go into the house,
greet your wife,
pick up your child, ask: *what's for dinner?*

I would like there to be a full-length mirror in your bedroom,
so that at the exact moment you turned off the light
my eyes looked at you through the mirror.

Behboodi Street

It is a time of mourning.
The young are in jail
and the mills are turning with blood,
the wine press is empty of red grapes.

It is a time of mourning.
The young are on the gallows
and the mills are turning with blood,
the wine press is empty of white grapes.

I crossed over the Kâshmar Plain.
Heads were scattered in every direction.
I passed through the Balkh Meadows.
Bodies were heaped in Hâmoon Lake.
I gave vent to a bitter song.
The mills were turning with blood.

I crossed the river, crossed the desert,
I crossed the burnt mountain,
I crossed the bolting plain.
On the horizon, the sky is blue.

In my sleep I saw a bloodied axe.
In my sleep I saw a white rope.
In my sleep I saw a clean garment.
I rolled from one dream into another.
Sleep stole my dreams.

In my sleep I saw a slaughtered camel.
In my sleep I saw a beheaded sheep.
A white swan flew from my chest.

The night reached its midst and the time for sleep arrived.
I tore my clothes.
Dishevelled my hair.
Took up residence in the alley.

From nightfall till morning, my desk was heard weeping.

The Dining Hall

I would like to live long enough
to go back one day to Mashhad,
to 13/1 Koohsangee Street.
To knock at the little window
for the green-hatted Sayyed to open the door.
To enter,
to see all of you in the dining hall
eating and telling jokes,
each of your faces unique.
One of you has a sick wife
and another has lost his father.
Someone's daughter has a new suitor,
another's son has been admitted to college.
A neighbour's child has fallen down the stairs
and you've bought a new TV.

I'd like to watch you
and look into your eyes.

The Old Warrior

I was the gardener here for forty years, Crow –
remember that.
Tell them to plant a tree in my memory at this corner
and a red rosebush.
In the shade of the tree, a wooden bench,
and on the bench, a plaque in my name:
No one may sit on this bench except for lovers
and nothing may be drunk here except red wine.

Thus said Alireza Abiz,
that old warrior.

Don't Let Go

The doors of the house open and we rush inside.
I light a cigarette to blow smoke in the eyes of a middle-aged
man.
An elderly lady appears on the veranda.

Like a tightrope walker I am unbalanced.

On the building site opposite, workers are carrying bricks.
A teenage boy siphons petrol from a motorcycle.
Black smoke rises from burning bins.

Hold my hand and don't let go.
Don't let go of my hand in the dark back alleys.

Legends

I am sitting in *Legends*
in a dark corner of the bar,
nursing a glass of beer
and thinking
in a hundred years – just one hundred years –
none of these people will be alive.

Not that one up there on the little stage
playing a new track every few minutes,
nor those young boys and girls skilfully filling glasses
and taking money,
nor this crowd moving their bodies unrhythmically.

And not me
– the melancholic scribbler of these lines –
the almighty god of these words.
Not one of us will continue to be,
we'll all be lost in legends.

From the window of my basement room
only the topmost wintry boughs are visible.
I hear the crying of the crows.
A cold morning envelops me.
In the mirror another man looks at me
with puffy eyes and white hairs in his temples,
a two-day beard.
He says: *Look at the world with fresh eyes.*
Tomorrow night there's a seminar, 'Rejuvenate with Love', in
        the Methodist church,
'People of all faiths and no faith welcome'.
The man in the mirror asks me in English: *What is your faith?*

I reply: *Speak in your mother tongue.*
With the words that you carry in your mind from the distant past.
Speak with the words of your ancestors.
Did my grandfather suffer any doubt in his faith?
Does my father ever think about his?

The world is too brief a space for thought.
The world is too brief an opportunity for thought.

A Dancing Wall

Last night in my dreams I composed a poem
like every night.
A translucent poem which shone upon me like a prism
I woke up and wrote down a line:
A dancing wall appeared before me
'A dancing wall appeared before me'
'A dancing wall'? why 'dancing'?
And why did it appear before me in English?
What was wrong with Persian?
What was marvellous about *a dancing wall*?
I who am a Persian poet
like Persian more.
There are plenty of walls in my memory.
In my Persian memory.

I was also a Persian poet in my dreams.
I was afraid to write in my diary.
I was afraid my roommate Ali Mostafayi
might betray me to the intelligence services.
I was afraid they might take me to Koohsangee Street,
to number 13/1.

The Orange Cloud

Does the man who throws himself under a train
think about what he is wearing?
Does he put on his best clothes?
Or whatever comes to hand?

Maybe he changes clothes again and again,
says to himself: *I've just bought this suit.*
This shirt is a better colour.
This sweater doesn't look good on me.
These shoes are scuffed.

Maybe he puts on an old jacket,
takes out his wallet and puts it in the drawer.
Writes a note leaving everything to his brother.
Maybe he smiles once in the mirror,
smokes a cigarette.
Looks for the last time at that orange cloud in the left-hand
        corner of the sky,
opens his mouth to the fine drops of rain,
and with the longing of a woman whose husband returns to
        her from war
leaps toward the train.

The Bowl of Milk

Then I told myself
think of more important things:
the leaf that fell from the branch,
the butterfly that escaped from the bowl of milk,
the breeze that suddenly blows at midnight,
and the fear of death.

The Border

The thin blue flame yawns
and falls off the fire.
Lies down for a while,
arches and stretches,
gathers strength and rises up dancing.

Darkness fills the valley,
and, over the border, the lights go on.

I Always Write That Which Is Not

I always write that which is not,
that which is defeats me.
I store it in the mind's attic
beneath odds and ends of memories
where I can't see it,
where it can't easily come to mind,
where it can rest and rot
in the soul's dark depths.

That which is is too terrifying
to wear the garment of the word.

The Pressure Gauge

Until this moment I had not thought
about the pressure gauge opposite,
but I have thought a lot
about Breyten Breytenbach,
and about his apology for his brilliant poem
to which he appended a list
of those who had lost their lives
as well as the name of their murderer:
Dear Prime Minister,
I honestly apologise.
Writing that poem was unjustified
as was its publication.

So, sincerely, to the dictator,
apologized Breyten Breytenbach,
poet.

Iftar

The girl opposite looked like my cousin.
We sat on the white cloth.
I was offered dates and took one.
Allah-u Akbar   *Allah-u Akbar*
Azan came to a close and Iftar began.
Allah-u Akbar   *Allah-u Akbar*
On the lips of those being shot
and on the lips of those doing the shooting.

Notes

'Puberty in the Trenches' (page 23)

The setting of this poem is Kurdistan, Iran during the early 1980s. Kurdish partisans, including the Komoleh Party, were fighting government forces. Palangân is a village on the foothills of Mount Shahoo. Dervish sects have a strong presence in this area. *Ghusle Janabat* is a ritual washing of the entire body by a Muslim after ejaculation or sexual gratification.

'To Shâh Cherâgh Shrine, All My Lemons' (page 27)

An allusion to verse 28, Chapter 13, Al Rad'd (Thunder) in the Quran which reads: 'Those who have believed and whose hearts are assured by the remembrance of Allah. Unquestionably, by the remembrance of Allah hearts are assured.'

'The Pressure Gauge' (page 70)

In 1975, Breyten Breytenbach, the South African poet and painter, returned from exile to his native country under a false name and carrying a false passport. He was arrested and tried for treason. On the stand during the trial, he apologised to the Prime Minister Balthazar Johannes Vorster for his poem entitled 'Letter from Abroad to the Butcher Balthazar' which he had published in the Netherlands in 1972. He said: "I would specifically like to apologize to the Prime Minister for a crass and insulting poem addressed to him. There was no justification for it. I am sorry".

Quoted from 'Breyten Breytenbach and the Censor' by J.M. Coetzee in *De-Scribing Empire, Post-Colonialism and Textuality*, edited by Chris Tiffin and Alan Lawson, Routledge, London and New York, 1994. p.86

Biographical Notes

ALIREZA ABIZ is a multi-award-winning Iranian poet, literary scholar, and translator. Born in South Khorasan, Iran in 1968, Abiz studied English Literature in Mashhad and Tehran universities and received his PhD in Creative Writing–Poetry from Newcastle University in the UK. Abiz has written extensively on Persian contemporary literature and culture. His scholarly book *Censorship of Literature in Post-Revolutionary Iran: Politics and Culture since 1979* was published in 2020 by I.B. Tauris / Bloomsbury. He has so far published five collections of poetry in Persian; *Stop! We Should Get Off!*, *Spaghetti with Mexican Sauce*, *I Hear My Desk as a Tree*, *13/1 Koohsangee Street*, and *Black Line – London Underground*. The latest collection published in 2017 was awarded the most prestigious independent poetry award in Iran, the Shamlou Award. His sixth collection, *The Desert Monitor*, will be published in 2021.

Abiz is has translated many leading poets including Rilke, Bunting, Walcott, Kerouac, and C.K. Williams into Persian. His translation of *African Contemporary Art* won him the Iranian Book of the Season Award for the best translation in visual arts in 2007. English, German and Arabic translations of his poetry have been published in numerous journals and anthologies and have been showcased in public places including Stuttgart subway in Germany. He has performed at many international festivals and acted as judge in numerous Persian language literary prizes. He is a board member of the Poetry Translation Centre and chaired the judges for the Sarah Maguire Poetry in Translation Prize 2020–2021.

Abiz is the co-founder of MAHA, a Persian-language online platform for art and literature and Editor of Radio Now podcasts. He lives in London where he works as a creative writing teacher, translator and researcher.

W.N. HERBERT is a highly versatile poet who writes both in English and Scots. Born in Dundee, he established his reputation with *Forked Tongue* (Bloodaxe,1994). This was followed by six further collections with Bloodaxe, most recently *The Wreck of the Fathership* (2020). He has also published a critical study, *To Circumjack MacDiarmid* (OUP, 1992), drawn from his PhD research. He co-edited *Strong Words: modern poets on modern poetry* (Bloodaxe Books, 2000) with Matthew Hollis, and his practical guide, *Writing Poetry*, was published by Routledge in 2010.

He has worked on collaborative translation from languages including Bulgarian, Chinese, Dutch, and Somali, editing *A Balkan Exchange* (Arc, 2007); *Jade Ladder* (Bloodaxe, 2012) and *The Third Shore* (Shearsman, 2013) with Yang Lian; and, with Said Jama Hussein, *So At One With You* (Poetry Translation Centre/ Ponte Invisible, 2018). He is currently working with Francis Jones and Fiona Sampson on *Collaborative Poetry Translation*, a critical study forthcoming from Taylor & Francis.

He is Professor of Poetry and Creative Writing at Newcastle University and lives in a lighthouse overlooking the River Tyne at North Shields. He was Dundee's inaugural Makar from 2013 to 2018. In 2014 he was awarded a Cholmondeley Prize, and an honorary doctorate from Dundee University. In 2015 he became a Fellow of the Royal Society of Literature.